Pioneers From the Past

Trailblazing Tales of Scientists and Innovators

Pankaj Madhukar

To my dearest children,

May your curiosity always be as boundless as the universe and may these stories of remarkable scientists kindle the flame of wonder within your heart. In your journey of exploration, may you find inspiration in the tales of those who dared to dream, challenged the norms, and illuminated the path for future generations. Here's to the joy of discovery and the magic that unfolds when we embrace the wonders of science.

With all my love,

Pankaj Madhukar

Contents

Preface

In the annals of history, there exist luminous narratives that transcend time, weaving tales of extraordinary individuals who, against all odds, shaped the course of humanity. The following pages unveil the illuminating journey of Edison, the pioneering radiance of Madame Curie, the uncharted symphony of Graham Bell, the mind beyond time embodied by Albert Einstein, and the vaccination revolution brought forth by Edward Jenner. These narratives are not just chronicles of scientific achievement; they are sagas of resilience, passion, and the relentless pursuit of knowledge.

Each story begins with a glimpse into the formative years of these exceptional minds, hinting at the challenges and peculiarities that marked their early lives. Edison, misunderstood as a child, found solace and guidance within the walls of his mother's homeschooling sanctuary. Madame Curie, a dreamer in Warsaw, defied societal expectations to delve into the mysteries of science. Graham Bell, deeply connected to his deaf mother, embarked on a quest to bridge the gap of communication. Einstein, a curious child in Ulm, Germany, pondered the universe's mysteries from a young age. Jenner, a keen observer in Berkeley, England, laid the groundwork for the revolutionary field of immunization.

As these individuals matured, their paths meandered through the intricate landscapes of curiosity, experimentation, and perseverance. Edison's entrepreneurial spirit ignited during adolescence, leading him to transform failures into stepping stones. Madame Curie's groundbreaking work with radium and polonium emerged from the toil of countless hours in a dimly lit laboratory. Bell's journey unfolded as an exploration of sound, culminating in the creation of the telephone that transformed communication. Einstein's "miracle year" of 1905 saw the birth of groundbreaking theories that reshaped the understanding of physics. Jenner's courageous experiment with cowpox laid the foundation for modern immunology.

The stories also delve into the personal lives of these luminaries, exploring the familial bonds, friendships, and mentors that shaped their character. Edison found an anchor in his mother, Madame Curie forged a profound friendship with Pierre, Bell collaborated with Thomas Watson, Einstein stood as a symbol of wisdom, and Jenner's experiment was realized with the consent of a courageous milkmaid and a young boy.

Beyond the scientific achievements, these narratives resonate with universal themes – the power of belief, the acceptance of differences, the importance of resilience, and the pursuit of dreams. Each story prompts reflection on the untold stories within our own pursuits, inviting us to embrace our uniqueness and unravel the extraordinary within.

Join us on this captivating journey through time and discovery, where the symphony of human ingenuity plays out in the lives of Edison, Madame Curie, Graham Bell, Einstein, and Jenner. As we turn the pages, may we be inspired to navigate our own uncharted territories and illuminate the world with the brilliance of our potential.

Pankaj Madhukar
25-12-2023

The Illuminating Journey of Edison

Thomas Alva Edison, a quintessential American inventor, etched his name in history with a world-record 1,093 patents. However, during his childhood he was a puzzle to his teachers. "What's to become of that boy?" they would whisper, shaking their heads. The classrooms echoed with their doubts. Little did they know that within Edison's seemingly troubled mind lay the seeds of brilliance, waiting for the right conditions to bloom.

Edison was the seventh and last child—the fourth surviving—of Samuel Edison, Jr., and Nancy Elliot Edison. At an early age, he developed hearing problems. He was imaginative and inquisitive, but, because in schools, much instruction was by rote, he was bored and was labelled a misfit. To compensate, he became an avid and omnivorous reader.

His mother, Nancy, a woman with a teacher's heart, saw beyond the labels and decided to homeschool him. "Thomas, my dear, the world may not understand you now, but I see a fire in you that can't be extinguished by the judgments of others," she said, her eyes filled with unwavering belief.

Their home transformed into a sanctuary of learning, filled with books and resources. "Mama, why do the others think I'm dumb?" young Edison questioned, his eyes searching for answers. "Thomas, you're not dumb; you're different. And that difference is your strength," Nancy replied, her words like a gentle breeze guiding him through the storm.

As adolescence dawned, Edison's entrepreneurial spirit ignited. With a glint in his eye, he said to his mother, "I want to try selling newspapers on trains, Mama. What do you think?" Nancy smiled, "I think it's a wonderful idea, my boy. Remember, success is not avoiding failure but learning from it."

Through business failures and disappointments, Nancy remained his anchor. "Mama, why do I keep failing?" Edison questioned, frustration etched on his face. "Failure is not the end, Thomas. It's a stepping stone to success. Each stumble is a lesson, a guide towards your true path," she reassured him, her wisdom shaping his perspective.

When the idea of creating a practical electric light bulb consumed him, Edison faced skepticism. "It's impossible, Edison. You're wasting your time," critics jeered. "Perhaps, but what if it's not?" Edison mused, his eyes filled with determination. His mother's voice echoed in his mind, "Believe in the impossible, my son, and make it possible."

In the laboratories of Menlo Park, New Jersey, Edison's team worked tirelessly. "We've tried a thousand filaments, Edison. It's not working," a team member lamented. Edison, undeterred, replied, "We haven't failed; we've simply found a thousand ways that won't work."

Finally, the eureka moment arrived. The glow of the incandescent light bulb illuminated not only the laboratory but also Edison's journey from a misunderstood boy to a visionary inventor.

As we ponder over Edison's story, we're left with a lingering question: What if our differences are not obstacles but the very keys to unlocking our greatest potential?

Pioneering Radiance in Science

In the late 19th century, a tenacious scientist set forth on a transformative journey that would reshape the scientific landscape. Born in Poland, Maria Skłodowska faced myriad challenges as she immersed herself in the mysteries of the unseen. Collaborating with her husband, they worked tirelessly in a small, dimly lit laboratory, fuelled by an insatiable curiosity.

Their focus centered on pitchblende, a peculiar mineral rumoured to harbour hidden secrets. Day after day, they painstakingly processed tons of this unassuming substance, hoping to extract something extraordinary. The process proved gruelling, with resources in short supply, yet their perseverance knew no bounds.

Amidst the clutter of beakers and test tubes, a breakthrough emerged. A faint glow, invisible to the naked eye, revealed the presence of something previously unknown to humankind. Little did the world know that this glow held the key to an entirely new realm of understanding.

Tragedy struck with the untimely death of Maria's husband, leaving her to carry on their quest alone. Undeterred, she forged ahead, unravelling the secrets hidden within the pitchblende. The culmination of her tireless efforts resulted in the discovery of radium and polonium, elements that defied the conventional wisdom of the time.

Recognition for her groundbreaking work arrived in 1903 with a Nobel Prize in Physics, shared with another scientist. Undaunted by adversity, Maria pressed on, earning yet another Nobel Prize, this time in Chemistry, in 1911.

And so, the determined scientist who unveiled the mysteries of radioactivity, defying the constraints of her era, was none other than the indomitable Madame Curie.

Maria Skłodowska, or Madame Curie as the world would come to know her, was a simple girl living in the vibrant city of Warsaw. Even in her early days, she was different—a dreamer with an insatiable curiosity that set her apart. Her family struggled financially, but within the walls of their modest home, Maria found solace in old books and the thrill of scientific discovery.

"Maria, you're a dreamer," her father would remark, perplexed by her constant questions. Unbeknownst to him, within those dreams were the seeds of groundbreaking discoveries. Maria's mother, however, saw the spark of brilliance in her daughter. "One day, everyone will see how smart you are," she reassured Maria, instilling a belief that would carry her through life.

As Maria grew, so did her thirst for knowledge. Despite societal expectations, she chose to defy the norm and pursue higher education at the Sorbonne in Paris. "Girls can't be scientists," people whispered. But Maria paid no mind, engrossed in her studies of physics and chemistry.

It was at the Sorbonne that she encountered Pierre Curie, a fellow scientist captivated by her intellect. "Your mind is like a universe waiting to be explored," he said, setting the stage for a partnership that would rewrite scientific history.

The Curies embarked on the daring exploration of radioactivity, facing numerous challenges. "Isolating radium and polonium is an arduous task," Pierre remarked. Maria, undeterred, replied, "True, but the pursuit of knowledge is worth every challenge."

Their groundbreaking work, however, faced skepticism. "A woman cannot win a Nobel Prize," critics scoffed. But the Curies, fueled by their love for science, pressed on. In 1903, they defied expectations by sharing the Nobel Prize in Physics with Henri Becquerel.

Tragedy struck with Pierre's untimely death, but Maria's spirit remained unbroken. "Pierre's legacy lives on in our work," she declared, becoming the first woman to win a Nobel Prize in two different fields.

Amidst the challenges, smaller stories unfolded. There were late-night experiments, fueled by passion and curiosity. There were moments of laughter in the laboratory, breaking the seriousness of scientific pursuits. And there were whispers of encouragement exchanged between Maria and Pierre during their toughest times.

As the glow of radium illuminated their lab, Maria's journey from a dreamer in Warsaw to a pioneering scientist became a series of smaller tales—a collection of moments that defined her resilience and passion. Her discoveries not only revolutionized medicine but also became the foundation of modern physics.

Madame Curie's story isn't just about science; it's a narrative woven with smaller stories of passion, determination, and the courage to challenge societal norms. It prompts us to reflect on the countless untold stories within our own pursuits and leaves us wondering what remarkable tales could unfold if we embrace our dreams with unwavering belief.

The Uncharted Symphony of Graham Bell

In the enchanting city of Edinburgh, where cobblestone streets whispered with the dreams of the young and the curious, Alexander Graham Bell emerged as a spirited and inquisitive boy. His fascination with the symphony of sound went beyond scientific curiosity; it was a journey sparked by a profound connection to his mother, Eliza, who was deaf and can't hear anything.

Their home, where the language of the heart transcended spoken words, became the crucible of Bell's childhood. Eliza became a guiding light for young Alexander. Despite her deafness, Eliza instilled in her son the belief that every challenge was an opportunity waiting to be embraced. Her hands painted a canvas of encouragement, fuelling Alexander's determination. This familial connection laid the foundation for his lifelong quest—to find ways for the deaf to connect with the world of sound and language.

Guided by his father Melville, who recognized the spark within his son, young Bell embarked on a journey into the realm of invention. Melville's words, "Every new idea is an adventure waiting to happen, Alex," ignited the flames of curiosity in the budding inventor.

Bell's expedition into the transmission of sound unfolded as a captivating adventure. "What if we could speak to someone far away, just like we do in the same room?" he pondered. The quest for a "talking machine" became an exploration of experimentation and discovery, a voyage that would alter the course of communication history.

In Boston, Bell's path intersected with that of Thomas Watson, a kindred spirit in the world of invention. Together, they transformed Bell's dream into reality. On a fateful day, as they tested their invention, Bell uttered the now-famous words, "Mr. Watson, come here, I want to see you." The voice had traversed the wires, marking the triumphant birth of the telephone.

Beyond the initial skepticism, Bell's invention revolutionized communication. However, his story extended beyond the telephone; it was the metamorphosis of a young boy's dream into a world-changing reality. Along the path, there were countless moments of trial and error, late-night experiments, and the unwavering support of his family.

In the expanding melody of the telephone's reach, Bell's message to children became clear: "Never be afraid to dream. Your ideas have the power to change the world." His story became an invitation for young minds to embrace challenges, turn them into adventures, and, like Bell, uncover the extraordinary within the seemingly ordinary.

Amidst the echoes of invention, another chapter unfurled in Bell's life—his connection with Helen Keller, a remarkable woman who triumphed over being deaf-blind to become an influential author and activist. This association began in Keller's early childhood.

Helen Keller, born in 1880 in Tuscumbia, Alabama, faced the challenges of deafness and blindness at the tender age of 19 months. A period of frustration and isolation followed until Anne Sullivan, Keller's devoted teacher, entered her life. Under

Sullivan's patient guidance, Keller learned to communicate through finger-spelling and tactile sign language.

During this pivotal time, Keller's parents sought advice from Alexander Graham Bell. Deeply engaged in communication for the deaf, Bell suggested reaching out to the Perkins Institute for the Blind in Boston, where Sullivan had received her training. Initially an advisor, Bell's involvement with Keller evolved into a profound friendship.

Understanding the challenges faced by the deaf, Bell, who had worked extensively with the deaf community, including his own mother and wife, recognized the potential in young Helen Keller. He believed that her education could be transformative.

With Bell's unwavering encouragement, Helen Keller's education flourished. Their relationship extended beyond formal education; they remained lifelong friends. Bell supported Keller in various ways, and his influence left a lasting impact on her development.

More than just a mentor teaching Keller to speak, Alexander Graham Bell became a steadfast friend and supporter, leaving an indelible mark on her life. Their enduring relationship showcased Bell's commitment to improving communication and education for individuals with sensory impairments.

And so, the tale of Alexander Graham Bell became an even richer narrative, interwoven with threads of personal challenges, unexpected turns, and the symphony of diverse interests that extended far beyond the wires of his most famous invention. It was a story that echoed not only across telephone lines but also through the hearts of children, inspiring them to believe that their dreams, like Bell's, have the power to resonate across the world, connecting people in ways they never imagined.

A Mind Beyond Time

Once upon a time, in the early 20th century, there was a brilliant physicist whose groundbreaking theories captured the world's attention. One day, a persistent reporter managed to secure an interview with this renowned scientist.

Eager to unravel the complexities of the physicist's mind, the reporter asked probing questions about theories and equations. The physicist, recognizing the enthusiasm, decided to simplify the explanation.

"Imagine putting your hand on a hot stove for a minute. It feels like an hour," the physicist began. "Now, picture sitting with a captivating companion for an hour. It feels like a mere minute. That's relativity."

As the words lingered in the air, the reporter absorbed the simplicity and elegance of the explanation. The physicist's ability to distill complex ideas into relatable anecdotes left a lasting impression on the reporter.

And so, the brilliant mind behind this insightful take on relativity was none other than Albert Einstein, the iconic scientist whose wit and wisdom transcended the boundaries of science.

 Albert Einstein was born on March 14, 1879, in the charming town of Ulm, Germany. His parents, Hermann and Pauline Einstein never imagined that their son would grow up to become one of the greatest minds in the history of science.

Young Albert was a bit different from other children. He didn't speak until he was three years old, causing some concern among his family. Little did they know that this delay was a precursor to the extraordinary way his mind worked.

As a child, Albert was curious about the world around him. His inquisitive nature often led him to question things that others took for granted. He would wonder what it would be like to ride on a beam of light or to catch up with time itself.

At the age of five, Albert received a compass as a gift, and this small, magnetic wonder ignited a spark within him. The needle's movement fascinated him, and he spent hours contemplating the invisible forces that guided it. This simple gift marked the beginning of his lifelong fascination with the mysteries of the universe.

Albert's formal education began in Munich, where his family had moved. School, however, was not a place where his unconventional thinking thrived. The rigid structure of the educational system clashed with his free-spirited mind. His teachers saw him as a rebellious student, often challenging authority and questioning the established norms.

Despite his early struggles in school, Albert's passion for learning persisted. He continued his education in Switzerland, where he enrolled in the Zurich Polytechnic. Here, he met Mileva Maric, a fellow student who would later become his first wife. Together, they faced the challenges of student life and nurtured their shared love for physics.

The year 1905 proved to be a turning point for Albert. In what would be known as his "miracle year," he published four groundbreaking papers that would forever alter the course of physics. One of these papers introduced the famous equation $E=mc^2$, unraveling the relationship between energy and mass.

As his fame grew, so did his commitment to social justice and pacifism. Einstein, now a renowned physicist, found himself thrust into the limelight. The world listened as he spoke out against war, injustice, and prejudice. He became a symbol of wisdom, compassion, and a tireless advocate for a better world.

In 1921, Albert Einstein received the Nobel Prize in Physics for his explanation of the photoelectric effect. However, he didn't rest on his laurels. The turbulent times of the 1930s and 1940s saw Einstein immigrating to the United States, fleeing the rise of the Nazi regime in Germany.

Einstein continued his scientific pursuits and became an American citizen. He collaborated with other brilliant minds, including his famous debates with Niels Bohr on the fundamental nature of reality. Einstein's unyielding curiosity and determination to understand the universe remained undiminished.

The latter part of his life was marked by a quest for a unified theory—a theory that would explain all the fundamental forces of nature. Although he never realized this dream, his contributions to science, humanity, and the understanding of the cosmos were immeasurable.

Albert Einstein passed away on April 18, 1955, leaving behind a legacy that transcends the realms of science. His story is not just one of brilliant equations and groundbreaking theories but a testament to the power of curiosity, perseverance, and the ability of one individual to change the world.

The Vaccination Revolution

In our world today, the thought of life without vaccinations is hard to imagine. As soon as a child is born, vaccinations protect them from serious diseases. It's not an exaggeration to say that human life often starts with vaccination. However, in the 18th century and earlier, this wasn't the case. Deadly diseases were common and affected entire societies. Smallpox was one such disease. It was highly contagious and lethal, claiming the lives of an estimated 400,000 people annually in Europe. Thirty percent of those who contracted it did not survive, and survivors often faced the risk of blindness.

Amidst this atmosphere of fear, a child emerged with keen observations and a curious mind, weaving a narrative of hope. Notably, he observed that milkmaids who had contracted a mild disease common among cattle, called cowpox, appeared to be immune to smallpox. This seemingly innocuous observation planted the seed of an idea that would later revolutionize the field of medicine. The name of this boy was Edward Jenner who later was regarded as father of immunization.

Edward was born in the quaint village of Berkeley, England in 1749. As Edward grew, his curiosity evolved into a passion for science and medicine. Apprenticing under a local surgeon, he acquired healing skills and knowledge that would shape his future. His inquisitive nature led him back to the intriguing connection between cowpox and smallpox.

In 1796, armed with his childhood observations and a bold hypothesis, Edward Jenner decided to test his theory through an experiment. He approached a milkmaid named Sarah Nelmes, who had recently contracted cowpox, seeking her consent for the experiment. After her approval, Jenner sought a suitable individual to inoculate with the cowpox-related germs.

After careful consideration, he chose to conduct his experiments on a child, as it was believed that children's developing immune systems would respond more robustly. Eventually, he successfully convinced the parents of a young boy named James Phipps to participate in the experiment. Jenner injected James with material from Sarah's hand lesions.

To Edward's relief and excitement, James developed a mild case of the disease but, crucially, showed no signs of smallpox when intentionally exposed to it later. This groundbreaking experiment marked the birth of a preventive method that would save countless lives.

Edward's revolutionary idea faced skepticism from the medical community initially, but the undeniable success of his experiment gradually won over supporters. The term "vaccination," derived from the Latin word meaning related to the original disease, highlighted the link between the two.

As news of Edward's discovery spread, the practice gained acceptance, becoming a cornerstone in the fight against the more severe ailment. Edward's pioneering work laid the foundation for modern immunology.

In the years that followed, Edward continued his research and advocacy for this preventive method, dedicating himself to the noble cause of saving lives. His innovation not only transformed medicine but also set the stage for future breakthroughs in preventing infectious diseases.

Reflecting on this story, we appreciate the profound impact a curious mind and a willingness to challenge the status quo can have on human history. The legacy of this pioneering scientist, Edward Jenner, lives on as a testament to the power of observation, experimentation, and the pursuit of knowledge for the betterment of humanity.

The Handwashing Pioneer

Dr. Ignaz Semmelweis, born on July 1, 1818, in Buda, Hungary, emerged as a pioneering figure in the field of medicine during the 19th century. His life story is marked by dedication, innovation, and a relentless pursuit of truth in the face of opposition.

Semmelweis began his journey into medicine by enrolling at the University of Vienna in 1837. He studied law initially but eventually switched to medicine, obtaining his doctorate in 1844. His early exposure to the medical field sparked a curiosity that would shape his future endeavours.

Semmelweis's career took a decisive turn when he joined the Vienna General Hospital in 1846. It was here that he encountered the mystery of puerperal fever, a devastating illness claiming the lives of numerous women in maternity wards. Disturbed by the stark contrast in mortality rates between two clinics, Semmelweis dedicated himself to uncovering the root cause.

In a groundbreaking move, Semmelweis introduced a simple yet revolutionary practice: handwashing with a chlorinated lime solution. He observed that the mortality rate significantly decreased when medical personnel washed their hands before attending to patients, particularly before childbirth. Despite initial skepticism and resistance from colleagues, Semmelweis persisted in advocating for this fundamental change in hygiene practices.

Semmelweis faced significant challenges in gaining acceptance for his ideas. The prevailing medical theories of the time, rooted in miasma theory, clashed with his emphasis on the importance of cleanliness. His colleagues were slow to embrace the notion that something as basic as handwashing could yield such profound results.

Despite his struggles, Semmelweis's handwashing protocol proved highly effective, saving lives and preventing the spread of infectious diseases. His work laid the groundwork for modern antiseptic practices. Unfortunately, his contributions were not fully recognized during his lifetime.

As Semmelweis sought to disseminate his findings, he faced rejection and criticism from the medical establishment. His passionate advocacy for handwashing led to strained relationships and isolation. Tragically, Semmelweis's mental health deteriorated, and he was committed to a mental institution in 1865, where he died at the age of 47.

Dr. Ignaz Semmelweis's life offers valuable lessons for the current generation. His story emphasizes the importance of challenging conventional wisdom, embracing innovation, and persisting in the face of adversity. Semmelweis's commitment to evidence-based medicine and his advocacy for a simple, effective solution in hand hygiene continue to inspire healthcare professionals worldwide.

In commemorating Dr. Ignaz Semmelweis, we celebrate not only a medical pioneer but also a visionary whose legacy reminds us of the transformative power of ideas, even in the face of initial skepticism and opposition.

Alexander Fleming's Journey to Penicillin

In the bustling city of London, a Scottish biologist and pharmacologist, Alexander Fleming, played a pivotal role in the world of scientific discovery. Born on August 6, 1881, in Lochfield, Ayrshire, Scotland, Fleming's early life was shaped by his upbringing in a farming family. His insatiable curiosity and love for knowledge led him to pursue higher education in London, where he graduated with distinction from St. Mary's Hospital Medical School in 1906.

Fast forward to 1928, Dr. Fleming found himself amidst the hustle and bustle of a cluttered laboratory in London, fully immersed in his research pursuits. No stranger to the intricacies of scientific discovery, little did he anticipate that a single, serendipitous observation would forever alter the landscape of medicine.

On that fateful day, Dr. Fleming had been investigating the properties of bacteria, particularly the notorious Staphylococcus. Petri dishes were scattered across his workspace, each holding its own experiment. Little did he know that a simple act of forgetfulness would lead to one of the greatest medical breakthroughs of the 20th century.

As Dr. Fleming busily attended to his duties, an unexpected summons pulled him away from his laboratory. Duty called, and he left for a brief vacation, temporarily abandoning his experiments. In his absence, something extraordinary happened.

Meanwhile, back in the laboratory, unnoticed and untouched, a petri dish containing Staphylococcus bacteria sat exposed to the elements. Perhaps it was fate or just a stroke of luck, but a mold known as Penicillium had drifted in through an open window and made itself at home on Dr. Fleming's forgotten experiment.

Upon his return, Dr. Fleming was greeted by a peculiar sight. His once-teeming Staphylococcus colonies were now surrounded by a curious halo – a zone where the bacteria seemed to have met their demise. Perplexed, Dr. Fleming examined the dish more closely, and a revelation dawned upon him.

Intrigued and astounded, Dr. Fleming muttered to himself, "That's odd. The bacteria seem to have succumbed to something in the air. Could it be the mold?" He meticulously studied the mold and its effects, discovering that it exuded a substance that effectively killed a wide range of bacteria.

Excitement bubbled within him as he pondered the potential implications of this accidental find. "Could this be a new way to combat bacterial infections?" he wondered aloud. Driven by scientific curiosity, he delved deeper into the properties of this newfound mold and its antibacterial substance.

In the following months, Dr. Fleming identified the substance responsible for this miraculous antibacterial effect and named it penicillin. Recognizing its potential to revolutionize medicine, he tirelessly worked to refine and produce penicillin in larger quantities.

The story of penicillin's discovery is not just one of scientific brilliance, but also a tale of serendipity and the relentless pursuit of knowledge. Dr. Fleming's accidental encounter with the mold in his laboratory opened the door to a new era in medicine, where infections that were once fatal became treatable, thanks to the wonder drug, penicillin.

Percy Spencer's Microwave Odyssey

In 1945, something interesting happened in a lab where scientists were testing radar equipment. One of those scientist noticed that a peanut bar in his pocket started cooking on its own. This got him curious, so he decided to do more experiments.

He asked a boy to get some popcorn, and when they brought it close to the radar equipment, the popcorn popped everywhere. The next day, the scientist tried something even crazier. He took a kettle, cut a hole in it, and put an uncooked egg inside. Then, using the radar equipment, he cooked the egg. A person nearby got a surprise when the egg burst and splattered.

What this scientist found out was amazing – you could cook using special radio waves. And guess what? The scientist's name was Percy Spencer, the guy who made this cool discovery.

Percy Spencer was born in Howland, Maine, in 1894. His early life was marked by curiosity and a knack for tinkering with machines.

Growing up in a modest family, Spencer's journey into the realm of electronics began when he joined the Navy during World War I. His talent for innovation didn't go unnoticed, and soon, he found himself immersed in the world of radar technology. Little did he know that his experiences during the war would set the stage for a revolutionary invention.

After the war, Spencer joined the Raytheon Corporation, where he continued to delve into the intricacies of electronic devices. One fateful day in 1945, while working on a magnetron, a component of radar systems, Spencer made an observation that would change the way we cook forever.

As he stood in front of the magnetron, he noticed that the candy bar in his pocket had melted. This peculiar incident triggered an idea – could the microwaves emitted by the magnetron be used for cooking? Intrigued, Spencer set out to explore this concept.

In his makeshift laboratory, Spencer conducted experiments using popcorn and eggs. To his amazement, the popcorn popped, and the egg exploded – a testament to the transformative power of microwaves. Realizing the potential applications of this discovery, Spencer and his team at Raytheon worked tirelessly to refine the concept.

In 1947, Raytheon introduced the first commercially available microwave oven, aptly named the "Radarange." This invention revolutionized the way people approached cooking, offering a quick and efficient alternative to traditional methods.

Percy Spencer's journey from a curious child in Maine to a pioneer of microwave technology showcased the power of innovation and the ability to find inspiration in unexpected places. His accidental discovery in front of a magnetron not only changed the way we cook but also laid the foundation for a kitchen revolution that would touch households around the world. And so, thanks to Percy Spencer's inventive spirit, the microwave oven emerged as a transformative force in the culinary landscape, forever altering the way we experience the art of cooking.

Alan Turing's Journey of Brilliance and Imagination

Once upon a time, in the bustling city of London, there lived a brilliant mathematician and inventor named Alan Turing. Born on June 23, 1912, Alan showed an extraordinary love for numbers and puzzles from a very young age.

Growing up, Alan attended Sherborne School, where his talent for mathematics shone brightly. His mind was like a sponge, soaking up all the fascinating ideas in the world of numbers. Little did he know that his love for puzzles would lead him to play a crucial role in a secret mission during World War II.

When World War II began, Alan Turing was called upon to use his incredible brainpower to help the Allies – a group of countries fighting together for a common cause. The Allies, including the United Kingdom, the United States, and others, were fighting against the Axis powers, led by Germany, Italy, and Japan.

The enemies (Axis powers) used a mysterious machine called Enigma to send messages to communicate amongst each other. These messages were like puzzles, scrambled in a way that seemed impossible to solve. In order to defeat them, it was important for them to know the plans of axis powers. So it was important for them to intercept and make sense of the messages sent via enigma. This will help them be better prepared for any offensive enemies were planning. This will also help them to strategize and counter-attack enemies. So the task to decipher the intercepted messages from enigma was quite important. Alan Turing's team were given this responsibility.

Undeterred by the challenge, Alan Turing put on his thinking cap and gathered a team of clever minds at Bletchley Park. Together, they worked day and night to unravel the secrets of the Enigma machine. It was like solving the most gigantic puzzle the world had ever seen.

After many attempts and countless hours of hard work, Alan and his team invented a special machine called the Bombe. This magical machine helped decode the secret messages sent by the enemies. Alan Turing's brilliant mind and the Bombe played a crucial role in helping the Allies win the war.

After the war, Alan Turing didn't stop using his imagination. He dreamed of machines that could do all sorts of incredible things. He even came up with a magical idea called the Turing Machine, which was like a superhero of the computer world. This idea laid the groundwork for the amazing computers we use today.

Alan Turing's story is like a thrilling adventure full of puzzles, secret codes, and magical machines. His brilliant mind continues to inspire kids around the world to dream big and think differently. And so, the story of Alan Turing, the Codebreaker, lives on as a tale of courage, intelligence, and changing the world with the power of ideas.

The Inspiring Journey of CV Raman

From a young age, C. V. Raman displayed an insatiable curiosity and a deep love for science. Growing up in Trichinopoly, he was fascinated by the play of sunlight on the waters of the nearby Cauvery River. This early fascination with the interplay of light and water would later become a cornerstone of his groundbreaking research.

Raman's academic journey was marked by excellence. He pursued his education at Presidency College in Madras, where he stood out as a brilliant student in physics. His academic prowess laid the foundation for his future contributions to the world of science.

Joining the Indian Association for the Cultivation of Science (IACS) in Calcutta marked a turning point in Raman's life. Here, he immersed himself in scientific research, driven by an unwavering passion to explore the mysteries of the physical world. It was during this time that he initiated experiments that would lead to the discovery of the Raman Effect.

One day, during a train journey, Raman noticed a peculiar phenomenon through the window. The Mediterranean Sea appeared to exhibit a mesmerizing blue color. Intrigued by this unexpected sight, Raman's scientific curiosity was piqued. He delved into an investigation, determined to understand the cause behind this phenomenon.

His keen observations and subsequent experiments revealed that the blue color of the sea was a result of the scattering of sunlight by water molecules. This seemingly simple yet profound observation not only showcased Raman's acute powers of observation but also laid the groundwork for his later work on the scattering of light and the discovery of the Raman Effect.

Raman's ability to turn a casual observation during a train journey into a scientific inquiry demonstrates his extraordinary capacity to find inspiration in the everyday world around him. It was moments like these that fueled his relentless pursuit of knowledge and shaped his innovative approach to scientific exploration.

In 1928, while investigating the scattering of light, Raman made a revolutionary discovery. He observed that when light passes through a transparent material, a small portion of it changes its wavelength. This phenomenon, known as the Raman Effect, was a groundbreaking revelation in the world of physics.

Raman's experiments were conducted with minimal equipment, often crafted by himself or his team, showcasing his resourcefulness. He believed, "The essence of Science is independent thinking, hard work, and not equipment. When I got my Nobel Prize, I had spent hardly 200 rupees on my equipment." This belief underscores his emphasis on intellectual curiosity and hard work over expensive resources.

In 1930, C. V. Raman was awarded the Nobel Prize in Physics for his work on the scattering of light. This prestigious recognition was not only a personal triumph but also a momentous occasion for Indian science. Raman became the first Asian and the first non-white person to receive a Nobel Prize in the sciences.

Throughout his career, Raman demonstrated a deep commitment to scientific education. He held various academic positions, including the Director of the Indian Institute of Science in Bangalore. His efforts to nurture and inspire the next generation of scientists left an enduring impact on scientific education in India.

C. V. Raman's life is a testament to the power of curiosity, perseverance, and a genuine love for knowledge. His ability to turn childhood curiosity into groundbreaking scientific discoveries, despite financial constraints, serves as an inspiration for young minds today. Raman's journey encourages aspiring scientists to follow their passions, ask bold questions, and contribute to the world of knowledge.

Stargazing Against the Odds

Once upon a time in Hanover, Germany, there lived a girl named Caroline. She faced the harsh reality of life from an early age. She got really sick when she was just ten years old, and it stunted her growth. She never grew taller than 4 feet 3 inches! On top of that, she lost vision in one of her eyes because of her illness. This setback led her family to believe that she wouldn't do anything in her life. They believed no one would marry her, either. So, her mother felt it was best for her to train to be a house servant rather than becoming educated in accordance with her father's wishes.

Her father sometimes took advantage of her mother's absence by tutoring her individually, or including her in her brother's lessons, such as violin. Caroline was briefly allowed to learn dress making. She tried to learn sewing from a neighbour, but she couldn't do much because she had to do a lot of housework. They didn't want her to become a governess and be independent, so they told her not to learn French or any fancy sewing beyond what she could learn from neighbours.

If things weren't tough already, everything went wrong when Caroline's dad passed away. It was really hard for her because he was her biggest supporter. Around that time, her brothers lived in Bath, England. Seeing how sad Caroline was, they suggested she come to Bath and try singing for her brother William's church performances. So, on August 16, 1772, she left Hanover with her brother's help, even though her mom wasn't happy about it. During the trip to England, Caroline got her first taste of astronomy, learning about stars and telescopes.

Even though Caroline didn't quite fit in with the local crowd and didn't make many friends, her sincere dedication and hard work shone through. She finally got the chance to feed her hunger for learning, taking regular singing, English, and arithmetic lessons from her brother. Not stopping there, she added dance lessons from a local teacher to her schedule. She even learned to play the harpsichord.

Her sincerity and hard work paid off, and soon she became a crucial part of William's musical performances at small gatherings. With time, she rose to become the principal singer at his oratorio concerts. Her vocal talents gained her a strong reputation, and after an outstanding performance of Handel's Messiah in April 1778, she was offered a spot at the Birmingham festival, where she became the first soloist. But soon things changed.

When William decided to focus more on studying stars and planets, Caroline also gave up singing to help him with his astronomy work. Even though she didn't know anything about stars or telescopes at first, she learned by watching her brother and helping him with his research.

Caroline started by polishing mirrors for telescopes, but soon she was doing the tricky calculations that went along with her brother's observations. As she got more interested, she used a small telescope to explore the sky and make her own discoveries.

In 1787, the king recognized her hard work and gave her a yearly payment for helping as an assistant astronomer — she became the world's first professional female astronomer! The next year, she spotted a periodic comet, which was later named

35P/Herschel-Rigollet, making her the first woman astronomer to find a comet.

After her brother William passed away in 1822, Caroline went back to Hannover and finished cataloging 2,500 nebulae and many star clusters. In 1828, when she was 77, the Astronomical Society gave her a gold medal for her work. She lived for another 20 years and kept earning the respect and admiration of scientists and regular people alike. Her story shows that even if you start knowing nothing, with hard work and passion, you can achieve incredible things.

Caroline's journey from a small town in Germany to becoming the world's first professional female astronomer is nothing short of extraordinary. Despite facing illness, societal expectations, and the loss of her biggest supporter, she persevered with sincerity and hard work.

Her story teaches us that challenges and setbacks are not the end of the road but opportunities for growth and discovery. Caroline's dedication to learning, her willingness to adapt, and her passion for astronomy turned her life around. From being a singer to becoming an integral part of groundbreaking astronomical research, she defied expectations and left an indelible mark on history.

Caroline Herschel's tale is an inspiration to us all. It reminds us that with determination, curiosity, and hard work, we can overcome obstacles and reach for the stars, just like she did. So, let her story be a beacon of hope for anyone facing challenges — the universe is vast, and there's always room for those who dare to dream and work towards their goals.

A tale of curiosity and discovery

It all started in 1665. The world was battling with bubonic plague. The schools and colleges were closed. During this period, a young man found himself pondering the mysteries of nature in the quiet orchards of Lincolnshire. One day, as he sat beneath an apple tree, an apple fell, catching his attention. This seemingly ordinary event sparked an extraordinary idea in his mind. He wondered, "Why does the apple fall straight down? Why not sideways or upwards?" In that moment of curiosity, the concept of gravity began to unravel.

He realized that the same force pulling the apple towards the Earth was the force that kept the Moon in orbit and governed the motion of planets. This revelation marked the birth of his groundbreaking theory of universal gravitation. It was as if the universe had whispered its secrets to him through the gentle fall of an apple.

Returning to Cambridge in 1667, he delved into the world of mathematics and science, ultimately becoming a professor and contributing immensely to various fields. Only later did the world come to know him as Sir Isaac Newton.

Sir Isaac Newton came into the world on Christmas Day, 25 December 1642 (according to the Julian calendar then used in England, or 4 January 1643 according to the Gregorian calendar) at a small village in Lincolnshire. Sadly, his father, also named Isaac Newton, had passed away just three months before his birth. Born ahead of schedule, Newton was a tiny baby; his mother, Hannah Ayscough, once remarked that he could easily fit inside a quart mug. At the tender age of three, Newton's mother remarried and moved in with her new husband, leaving young Isaac in the care of his maternal grandmother.

From around twelve to seventeen years old, Newton went to The King's School in Grantham. They taught him Latin, Ancient Greek, and a bit of math. But by October 1659, he had to leave school and go back home. Newton's mom, who was a widow again, wanted him to be a farmer, but he really didn't like that idea. Luckily, a teacher named Henry Stokes from The King's School convinced Newton's mom to let him go back to school.

Newton went back, and this time, he became the best student. He did cool things like making sundials and models of windmills, and he was even a bit motivated by wanting to get back at a bully from school. That's how he showed everyone that he was really smart and creative.

In 1661, Newton got admitted to the University of Cambridge, but he didn't stand out as a great student at first. Then, in 1665, the school had to close temporarily because of a dangerous illness called bubonic plague. Newton went back home to Lincolnshire for two years, and it was during this time that he had the idea about apples falling from trees – a really smart thought that he considered the best time for inventing things.

Even though he liked studying on his own, Newton went back to Cambridge in 1667. From then until 1696, he worked there as a professor of mathematics and in other roles.

But there's more to Newton than just the apple idea! He also worked on calculus, a kind of math, along with a German mathematician named Gottfried Leibniz. They came up with some really important techniques that mathematicians and scientists still use today.

Newton was curious about light too. He figured out that white light is a mix of all the colors of the rainbow. This discovery explained why telescopes of that time didn't show colors properly. To fix this, Newton designed a telescope that used mirrors instead of just glass lenses. This improved telescope design is still used in many telescopes today, including the famous Hubble Space Telescope.

After thinking about falling apples, Newton went on to develop three important rules about how things move. He called them the laws of motion. So, from apples to laws of motion, Isaac Newton showed us that curiosity and thinking differently can change the world.

From Bicycles to Flight

Once upon a time in Dayton, Ohio, two brothers named Orville and Wilbur Wright were destined to change the course of history. Raised in a modest family, their lives revolved around the pursuit of knowledge and innovation.

The brothers, inseparable since childhood, were fascinated by the mysteries of flight. Their journey into aviation began with a simple toy – a model helicopter made of cork, bamboo, and paper, powered by a rubber band. The mesmerizing flight of this toy launched an obsession that would shape their entire lives.

 In 1878, the brothers' father tossed the toy into the air, and instead of falling as expected, it soared across the room. The sight captivated young Orville and Wilbur, sparking a passion for aviation that would eventually lead to the invention of the airplane.

The family moved from Indiana to Dayton in 1884, and it was here that the brothers spent the majority of their lives. Despite facing financial challenges, they embarked on various ventures, from a newspaper printing business to a bicycle repair shop, all fueled by their determination to explore the possibilities of flight.

In 1889, the brothers started a newspaper printing business, and by 1892, they had opened a bicycle repair shop. The success of their bicycle business funded their experiments in aviation. The brothers, neither of whom received a high school diploma or married, were wholly dedicated to their work.

The turning point came when they decided to build their own aircraft, the Wright Flyer I. In 1903, after numerous experiments and challenges, when they were ready to fly, they had to do a coin toss to decide who would be the first to fly. Orville and Wilbur had promised their father, who feared losing both sons in an airplane accident, they would never fly together. Orville won the coin toss to become the first to test the aircraft on the sandy grounds of Kill Devil Hills, North Carolina. His historic 12-second flight changed the world.

The aircraft they built, the Wright Flyer I, cost about $1,000 and was entirely financed by the brothers. It featured a framework made of spruce, twin "pusher" propellers, and a specially designed engine, casting the foundation for modern aviation.

Throughout their lives, the brothers adhered to their promise to their father, never flying together. The only exception was made on May 25, 1910, when Orville piloted while Wilbur, the passenger, experienced the thrill of flight. As Orville gained altitude, their excited father shouted, "Higher, Orville, higher!"

The Wright brothers' journey wasn't just about flying; it was about resilience, innovation, and a relentless pursuit of dreams. They faced skepticism, financial constraints, and the risk of failure, but their commitment to pushing the boundaries of human achievement remained unwavering.

The Wright brothers' legacy continues to soar, inspiring generations to come. Their story teaches us that curiosity, determination, and a bit of sibling rivalry can lead to groundbreaking achievements. As we board planes and traverse the skies today, let's remember the pioneers who defied gravity and taught the world to fly – Orville and Wilbur Wright.

The Extraordinary Journey of Robert H. Goddard

Robert H. Goddard was born on October 5 1882, in Worcester, Massachusetts. His eyes, filled with wonder and curiosity, often gazed up at the night sky, sparking a fascination with the mysteries beyond Earth. This boy, destined to become a trailblazer in rocketry, would forever alter the trajectory of space exploration.

From his earliest years, Goddard displayed an insatiable appetite for knowledge and a profound interest in science. His dreams extended far beyond the confines of his hometown, envisioning a future where space travel was made possible through rockets. Little did he know that these dreams, born in the imagination of a young boy, would shape a revolutionary chapter in human history.

Despite frequent battles with illnesses, Robert found solace in the world of books, spending countless hours at the local library. His frailty didn't define him; instead, it fueled his imagination and determination to reach for the seemingly unreachable.

Robert H. Goddard's journey into the realm of science began with a spark – a literal one. It was an ordinary day when his father, eager to share a bit of scientific wonder, demonstrated the creation of static electricity on the family's carpet.

Wide-eyed and filled with wonder, five-year-old Robert watched in amazement as the sparks danced around his father's fingertips. The magic of that moment ignited a flame of curiosity that would burn brightly throughout his life.

Inspired by this newfound fascination, Robert's young mind raced with possibilities. One day, armed with the knowledge imparted by his father, he embarked on a mission to unravel the mysteries of electricity. His grand experiment involved a seemingly simple question – could he jump higher with the help of charged zinc?

In his makeshift laboratory, which doubled as the family's gravel walk, Robert scuffed his feet energetically, aiming to charge the zinc from a battery. With each scuff, he imagined soaring through the air, defying gravity itself. However, reality had its way of tempering youthful ambitions. Much to his dismay, holding the charged zinc, he could jump no higher than usual.

Undeterred by this initial setback, Robert's experiments continued, fueled by an insatiable curiosity. His young mind, untamed by the constraints of convention, envisioned soaring to new heights – perhaps even beyond the clouds. That was until a gentle but cautionary voice interrupted his ambitious endeavors.

As he scuffed and charged the zinc once more, a warning echoed through the air – not from the crackling sparks but from his mother, a voice of reason in the midst of youthful exuberance. "If you succeed," she cautioned, "you might go sailing away and might not be able to come back."

The vivid imagery of a young boy sailing into the unknown, propelled by the very forces he sought to harness, lingered in the air. It was a mother's gentle reminder that every journey into the realms of the unknown carried both the thrill of discovery and the weight of responsibility.

With the wisdom of a parent, she gently nudged him to tread carefully, to dream boldly but to anchor those dreams in the soil of reality. The experiment may have been paused, but the spark of curiosity and the dream of soaring beyond never dimmed.

Little did Robert know that this early encounter with the wonders of electricity would be a prelude to a lifetime of groundbreaking experiments and a legacy that would leave an indelible mark on the annals of science. The boy who once sought to jump higher would, in time, propel humanity into the cosmos, touching the very stars that had ignited his childhood imagination.

Robert H. Goddard's journey into the vast realms of science and space was not a solitary endeavor but a guided odyssey, nurtured by the keen encouragement of his father. A crucial architect of Goddard's scientific curiosity, his father recognized the budding potential in his son and equipped him with the tools of exploration – a telescope, a microscope, and a subscription to the fascinating world of Scientific American.

Under the influence of these instruments, young Goddard's imagination took flight, quite literally. The concept of flight, an age-old dream, gripped his young mind, compelling him to explore the skies in unconventional ways. Kites and balloons became his vessels of discovery, each ascent a step closer to the heavens.

At the tender age of 16, fueled by an audacious spirit, Goddard set his sights on a grand experiment – constructing a balloon made entirely of aluminum. In the makeshift laboratory of his home workshop, the raw metal was shaped with determined hands. The project, though ending in failure, became a crucible for forging Goddard's growing determination and confidence.

His fascination with aerodynamics took flight as he studied the scientific papers of Samuel Langley, who observed birds' wing movements. Inspired by the grace of swallows and chimney swifts, Robert began to see the magic of flight in the gentle sway of feathers. A letter to St. Nicholas magazine, sharing his observations, revealed the spirit of a young dreamer who believed in the power of human intelligence to conquer the skies.

Robert's journey took a cosmic turn when he encountered Newton's laws of motion. Testing these laws on his own, he realized that the secrets of space were waiting to be unveiled through physics and mathematics. His notebooks, scribbled with calculations, became a testament to a young mind hungry for discovery.

In 1912, with determination as his guiding star, Robert independently developed the mathematics needed for rocketry, setting the stage for his groundbreaking work. Battling the adversity of tuberculosis in 1913, he refused to let illness extinguish the flames of his dreams. As he slowly recovered, he spent each day meticulously working on his notes, driven by an unyielding passion.

The fall of 1914 marked a turning point as Robert accepted a position at Clark University, where his dreams of rocketry could take flight. In 1915, against all odds, he launched the world's first powder rocket, a momentous event that echoed through the corridors of history.

Robert H. Goddard's journey inspires us, the current generation of dreamers and explorers. His story teaches us that dreams, no matter how audacious, can defy the limitations set by circumstances. His frailty didn't hinder his ascent to the stars; instead, it fueled his imagination and determination.

As we look up at the night sky, let's remember Robert H. Goddard – the boy who refused to be defined by his weaknesses and dared to dream beyond the stars. His legacy reminds us that within every child, there's a spark that can ignite the cosmos, and all it takes is belief, perseverance, and a little bit of rocket fuel for the journey ahead.

Vikram Sarabhai's Odyssey Beyond the Stars

Born on August 12, 1919, Sarabhai grew up with an insatiable curiosity and a fervent passion for science. Little did the world know that this young boy would blossom into one of India's most influential space scientists.

Vikram's journey began with a solid foundation in science and education. His parents, Ambalal and Sarla Devi Sarabhai, recognized his intellectual prowess early on and provided him with an environment that fostered learning. Vikram completed his early education in Gujarat and then ventured to Cambridge in the United Kingdom for higher studies.

His years at Cambridge were transformative, and he delved into the realms of cosmic rays and nuclear physics. The young scientist, armed with knowledge and a burning desire to contribute to his nation's progress, returned to India.

In 1947, as India gained independence, Vikram Sarabhai found himself at the crossroads of history. Instead of pursuing a lucrative career abroad, he chose to dedicate himself to his homeland. His vision extended far beyond the conventional, and he believed that India's future lay in harnessing the power of space technology.

In 1962, Vikram Sarabhai laid the foundation for the Indian National Committee for Space Research (INCOSPAR), which later evolved into the Indian Space Research Organisation (ISRO). His dream was to harness space technology for India's development, and against all odds, he paved the way for India's space odyssey.

One of his most significant contributions was the establishment of the Thumba Equatorial Rocket Launching Station (TERLS), a modest facility that played a pivotal role in India's early experiments with space exploration. The historic launch of India's first satellite, Aryabhata, in 1975 marked the realization of Sarabhai's dream.

Beyond his technical brilliance, Vikram Sarabhai possessed a rare quality – the ability to inspire and nurture talent. He recognized the potential of young scientists and engineers, encouraging them to push boundaries and dream big. Under his guidance, India's space program gained momentum, and the seeds he planted grew into a forest of achievements.

Tragically, Vikram Sarabhai's journey was cut short when he passed away on December 30, 1971, at the age of 52. However, his legacy lived on in the numerous satellites that orbited the Earth, connecting distant corners of the country and transforming communication and remote sensing.

Today, as we look up at the skies and witness the triumphs of ISRO – from Chandrayaan to Mangalyaan – we owe a debt of gratitude to the man who dared to dream beyond the stars. Vikram Sarabhai's life story teaches us that audacious dreams, coupled with unwavering determination, can propel a nation to new heights.

His legacy is an everlasting testament to the power of innovation, scientific temperament, and a relentless pursuit of excellence. Vikram Sarabhai, the father of India's space program, continues to inspire generations to reach for the stars and beyond.